ENJOYING PRAYER
STUDY GUIDE

Knowing God and Transforming the World

Matthew Lilley

©2024 by Matthew Lilley
All rights reserved. No part of this book may be used or reproduced in any manner whatsoever without written permission, except in the case of brief quotations in critical articles and reviews. For more information and permission, write to: inscribepress@gmail.com.

Published by Presence Pioneers Media, Farmville, NC
Cover design by Mary Beth Barefoot.
Contact her at marybethbarefoot@gmail.com.
Interior design by Jeffrey Pelton.
Printed in the United States of America.

ISBN 978-1-951611-59-0

Unless otherwise indicated, Scripture quotations are from The ESV® Bible (The Holy Bible, English Standard Version®), copyright © 2001 by Crossway, a publishing ministry of Good News Publishers. Used by permission. All rights reserved.

CONTENTS

How to use this Guide / 1

Part One: Foundations for Enjoyable Prayer
    Love: The Purpose of Prayer / 5
    Our Father: The Object of Prayer / 9
    Sonship: Our Identity in Prayer / 13
    First: The Priority of Prayer / 17

Part Two: Keys to Enjoyable Prayer
    Worship: Combining Music and Prayer / 23
    Scripture: The Language of Prayer / 27
    Listening: Hearing God's Voice in Prayer / 31
    Persistence: Staying Faithful in Prayer / 35

Part Three: Transformation Through Enjoyable Prayer
    Intercession: Partnership with God in Prayer / 41
    Tongues & Travail: Spirit-Filled Prayer / 45
    Fasting: Hunger for God Through Prayer / 49

Part Four: The House of Enjoyable Prayer
    Together: The Need for Corporate Prayer / 55
    Unceasing: A Movement of Day & Night Prayer / 59

Conclusion / 63

How to Use This Guide

Welcome to the Enjoying Prayer Study Guide. Whether you are participating as an individual or with a group, get ready to embark on an in-depth and life-changing study of Scripture around the topic of prayer.

Each chapter of the study guide corresponds to a chapter in the Enjoying Prayer book and to a video from the online course. To have the best experience, read one chapter of the book weekly, then meet in a small group to watch the video and discuss the study guide. It is also effective even if you choose just one — the book or the videos. This resource can also be used as a standalone guide for personal Bible study.

Each chapter of the study guide contains the following elements:

- **Big Idea.** This is a short quote from the *Enjoying Prayer* book summarizing the chapter.
- **Three Truths.** These are the three ideas, based in Scripture, that you will explore more deeply. Each truth is accompanied by Scripture to read and questions to answer. The bulk of your study time will be spent on this section.
- **Quote.** An inspirational quote from an outside source related to the chapter topic.
- **Word Study.** A deep dive into one of the Hebrew or Greek words used in a Bible verse from that chapter — providing even more illumination to the topic at hand.
- **Activation.** A practical activity for you to do on your own time. This helps you move from being knowers of the Word to doers of the Word.

Here are some suggestions on how to get the most out of this resource:

1. **Read and Watch First.** Read the chapter or watch the video before going through the corresponding study guide chapter.
2. **Go Analog.** Try to avoid using your phone or digital devices, as they can easily become a distraction.
3. **Bring your Bible.** Use your physical Bible to read the Scriptures.
4. **Write.** Write answers to the questions in the space underneath or in a separate journal. Writing down your answers (versus merely thinking about them) helps you process what you're studying more deeply and remember the truths you're learning in greater detail.
5. **Participate in the activations.** Do not skip this portion of the study. Many people find that this is when the truth you are reading and hearing will finally start to "click."

6. **Go Deeper.** Consider reading the books in the Further Reading sections to go even deeper into the topics that are particularly impactful to you.

The purpose of this study guide is life transformation. To get the most out of this transformation, be sure to engage fully with all aspects of the study guide. I guarantee that if you fully engage — honestly answering every question and doing the activations in this guide — your life will be changed!

Matthew Lilley

P.S. Before you start, go read the *Enjoying Prayer* book introduction and/or watch the introductory course video.

Part One:
Foundations for Enjoyable Prayer

Love: The Purpose of Prayer

Big idea: *"Prayer exists as a means to experience God's relational presence." (pg. 10)*

1. The purpose of prayer is love

   - Read John 3:16, 17:3. According to Jesus, what is eternal/everlasting life? When is it and where is it?

     _____

     _____

     _____

   - Read Matthew 22:35-40. Are some portions of the Bible more important than others? What is the most important verse in the Bible? Jesus emphasized the command in verse 37 as the "first" and "greatest" commandment; what does that say about God's nature and heart?

     _____

     _____

     _____

   - If God can do whatever He wants (Psalm 115:3), why would He want you to ask Him to do things?

     _____

     _____

     _____

ENJOYING PRAYER

2. God desires intimacy

- Read Song of Solomon 2:10-12. What does it mean to have "intimacy" with God in prayer? Does the concept cause you discomfort when talking about God? If so, why do you think that is the case?

  _____
  _____
  _____
  _____
  _____

- Read Matthew 25:1-13. Based on verse 12, what do you think the "oil" represents? How can you ensure that you have "oil in your lamp"?

  _____
  _____
  _____
  _____
  _____

3. Intimacy requires honesty

- Read Matthew 6:5-8. How can you be more honest in your prayer life? Are you scared to open your heart up to God and be truly vulnerable? If so, why?

  _____
  _____
  _____
  _____
  _____

> *"At the center of it all is God — the Triune God, who has created and redeemed and invited his people to enjoy his relational presence for eternity. That is what the Bible is all about."*
>
> J. Daniel Hays and J. Scott Duvall[1]

Word Study - "Love"

There are multiple Greek words translated "love" in the New Testament. Some of them indicate brotherly love or romantic affection. However, the word Jesus uses in Matthew 22 to describe how we should love Him is the word "**agapeo**" — the verb form of the Greek noun **agape**.

Agape is a unique kind of love that emphasizes "unconditional love, charity; the love of God for person and of person for God." In other words, God's command that we love (**agapeo**) Him requires that we first receive His unconditional love (**agape**) for us (I John 4:19).

Activation

Get a journal or notepad and write a brutally honest prayer to God. Don't self-edit or over-analyze. Just get raw and real as you open your heart to the Lord. Share your hopes, dreams, fears, and disappointments with Him.

Further Reading

The Pursuit of God by AW Tozer

Our Father: The Object of Prayer

Big idea: *"We must allow the truth of God as Father to set us free and draw us into joyful prayer." (pg. 24)*

1. In prayer we approach God as a loving Father.

   - Read Matthew 6:7. Why do you think Jesus wants you to approach God in prayer specifically as a Father?

     _____

     _____

     _____

     _____

   - How do you feel relating to God as a Father? Does this awaken positive or negative emotions for you? Why is that?

     _____

     _____

     _____

     _____

     _____

     _____

ENJOYING PRAYER

- What are some negative ways your earthly father's behavior makes it harder to relate to God as a Father? As needed, forgive your father, and repent of any lies you've believed about God.

  _____
  _____
  _____
  _____
  _____

2. A biblical view of the Father sets us free

- Read Luke 15:11-32. Focus on the father in the story first. What stands out to you about what he does and says? How does he treat the son who ran away? How does he treat the son who stayed at home? How does your Father treat you?

  _____
  _____
  _____
  _____
  _____

- Which of the two sons in the story do you relate to the most? What was the father trying to express to that son?

  _____
  _____
  _____
  _____
  _____

OUR FATHER: THE OBJECT OF PRAYER

- Read Zephaniah 3:17, Romans 5:8, and Romans 8:1. What do these verses communicate about God's heart and nature? What do they reveal about how God treats you?

_____
_____
_____
_____
_____
_____

3. Jesus wants us with Him in the Father's love

- Read Jesus' prayer for you in John 17:20-24. How does it make you feel that the Father loves you like He loves Jesus? How much does the Father love the Son (see Matthew 3:17)?

_____
_____
_____
_____
_____

- Read John 17:24 again. What is Jesus' burning desire?

_____
_____
_____
_____
_____
_____

ENJOYING PRAYER

> *"What comes to mind when we think about God is the most important thing about us."*
>
> — A.W. Tozer

Word Study - "Father"

In Matthew 6, Jesus teaches his disciples to address God as their Father. He uses the word twelve times throughout the chapter. The Greek word he uses is **pater**, which in Aramaic (Jesus' native language) is the word **Abba.** This word is found in Mark 14:36, Romans 8:15, and Galatians 4:6. The New Testament's use of **Abba** by Jesus and Paul shows us that we can speak to God naturally, personally, and intimately. Our English equivalent would be the way a child might informally refer to their father as "Daddy" or "Dad."

Activation

Take ten minutes to "soak" in the Father's love. Lie down and listen to the song "I Am Your Beloved" by Jonathan and Melissa Helser. Take deep breaths and receive the Father's love for you.

Further Reading

Experiencing Father's Embrace by Jack Frost

Sonship: Our Identity in Prayer

Big Idea: *"If God is Father, then you are a son or daughter." (pg. 32)*

1. Our identity in Christ is as sons and daughters

    - Read I John 3:1. Do you believe that you are a child of God? Is this central to your identity and sense of self? Does your sense of identity depend on praise and affirmation from others? Does your sense of identity crumble when you are criticized? Why or why not?

    _____

    _____

    _____

    _____

    _____

    _____

    - Read Matthew 3:17. If you are "in Christ" as a believer, what does this verse say about the Father's feelings towards you?

    _____

    _____

    _____

    _____

ENJOYING PRAYER

- Read Ephesians 3:16-19. What does it mean to be "rooted" and "grounded" in God's love?

_____

_____

_____

_____

2. We are both born again and adopted

- Read John 3:3-7. What does it mean to be "born again" (see also I Peter 1:23)? Why did Jesus choose the language of birth to describe following Him in faith?

_____

_____

_____

_____

- Read Romans 8:17, Galatians 3:29, and Titus 3:7. In an earthly family, what does it mean to be an "heir"? What makes someone a rightful heir? In the context of God's family, what does it mean that you are an heir of God's kingdom?

_____

_____

_____

_____

- Read Romans 8:15-17. Why does Paul use the language of adoption to describe your identity as God's child? What role does the Holy Spirit have in revealing your adoption as God's son or daughter (see Romans 5:5)? How does being adopted by God affect your daily life?

_____

SONSHIP: OUR IDENTITY IN PRAYER

_____
_____
_____
_____
_____
_____

3. We are no longer slaves or orphans

- Review Romans 8:15-17. In what ways do a "spirit of slavery" and a "spirit of adoption" contrast? How would a "spirit of slavery" manifest in your life? How would a "spirit of adoption" manifest in your life? How would these mindsets change your regular behavior and impact your closest relationships?

_____
_____
_____
_____
_____
_____

- Read John 14:18. What would be some of the characteristics of a spiritual "orphan"? Do you see any of those characteristics in your life? How exactly did Jesus "come" to us, as He promised in this verse?

_____
_____
_____
_____
_____

ENJOYING PRAYER

- Read 2 Corinthians 10:4-6. How does this passage encourage you to fight against the orphan and slave mindsets?

_____

_____

_____

_____

_____

> *"There is nothing you can do to cause God to love you any more than He does right now. There is nothing you can do to cause God to love you any less that He does right now."*
>
> — JACK FROST

Word Study - "Son"

In Hebrew culture, the first-born son is who would receive the inheritance from his father. The oldest male child was the rightful heir to the family estate. In Romans 8:14, Paul says that all Christians who receive the Holy Spirit are sons of God. The Greek for son is **huios** (Strong's G5207). Men *and* women who accept Christ become spiritual "sons" (**huios**) and are therefore rightful heirs in the kingdom of God.

Activation

Soaking part two. Take ten minutes, lie down, and listen to the song "So Proud Of You" by Andrew Ehrenzeller. Receive the love and affirmation of your Father. Accept your identity as a child of God.

Further Reading

Orphan Slave Son by Ben Pasley

First: The Priority of Prayer

Big idea: *"Your relationship with God is the most important thing in your life, and therefore — prayer being one of the primary ways you relate to God — prayer should be prioritized." (pg. 45)*

1. Abiding in Christ Produces a Fruitful Life

- Read John 15:4-5. How can you have a fruitful life? What does it mean to abide in Christ? What happens if you do not abide in Christ?

  _____

  _____

  _____

  _____

- Read John 15:7-11. How can you let Jesus' words abide in you? How can you abide in Jesus' love? What are the results of this abiding, according to this passage?

  _____

  _____

  _____

  _____

  _____

ENJOYING PRAYER

2. Praying First Positions Us to Obey the Father

- Read Luke 5:15-16. What does this passage tell you about Jesus' prayer life? Why did Jesus have to pray to the Father? According to these verses, how often did Jesus pray? How can Jesus' example impact your life?

- Read John 5:19. What does it mean that Jesus was only doing what the Father is doing? How did Jesus know what the Father was doing? How does Jesus' approach to life differ from yours? Do you only do what you see the Father doing?

- Read John 5:1-9. In light of verse 19, why do you think Jesus only healed the one man?

3. Prayer Precedes Power

- Read Acts 1:4-8. Why did Jesus tell his disciples to wait in prayer before they started their mission of preaching the Gospel?

FIRST: THE PRIORITY OF PRAYER

- Read Matthew 28:19-20. Why does Jesus tell his disciples to "go" in this passage, but in Acts 1 He tells them to "wait"? How do you know when to pray and when to do other things God has called you to do?

- Read Acts 6:1-6. What activity did the apostles delegate to others? What activity did they recommit to doing themselves? What was the result of their decision? What activities are getting in the way of your prayer life?

> *"I have so much to do that I shall spend the first three hours in prayer."*
>
> — Martin Luther

Word Study - "Devote"

In Acts 6:4, the apostles delegate some of their ministry work so that they can "devote" themselves to prayer and God's word. The Greek word translated "devote" is **proskartereō** (Strong's G4342), which means "to be steadfastly attentive unto, to give unremitting care to a thing." This kind of "unremitting care" is required if you want to prioritize prayer in your life and not get distracted from what is most important.

ENJOYING PRAYER

Activation

Set a time and place for prayer, and put it on your calendar. Most importantly: tell someone else what you're doing and ask them to follow up with you. Show up to your time and be with God.

Further Reading

Give No Rest! by Lee Cummings

Part Two:
Keys to Enjoyable Prayer

Worship: Combining Music and Prayer

Big idea: *"In God's presence there is fullness of joy, and we enter God's presence with praise. Therefore enjoyable prayer should be worship-based prayer."* *(pg. 66)*

1. God Loves Music

   - Read Zephaniah 3:17. Who is singing to whom? What does this indicate about God's nature and personality?

     _____

     _____

     _____

   - How many times does the Bible use the word sing, song, or music? (Try searching on biblegateway.com)

     _____

     _____

   - Read Revelation 5:8. What are the two things that the 24 elders hold in their hands? What does the incense represent? Why do you think God has musical instruments in His heavenly throne room?

     _____

     _____

     _____

     _____

ENJOYING PRAYER

2. Musical Praise Brings Us Into God's Presence

- Read Jesus' prayer in Matthew 6:9-13 in the New King James Version. What does it mean to "hallow God's name" and why should our prayers begin with hallowing? How does the prayer end? How does the beginning and end of the Lord's prayer inform how you should pray?

- Read Psalm 100:4. What activities bring you into the presence of God? Have you ever experienced God's manifest presence while thanking and praising Him?

- Read Psalm 22:3. What does this verse tell you about the power of praise? What does God inhabit; where is God enthroned?

WORSHIP: COMBINING MUSIC AND PRAYER

3. Combining Music and Prayer Brings Heaven to Earth

- Read Isaiah 56:7 and Psalm 16:11. What theme connects these two verses? How does Psalm 16:11 help you experience the joyful prayer promised in Isaiah 56:7?

  _____
  _____
  _____
  _____
  _____

- Read Matthew 6:10. What does Jesus say about heaven coming to earth? What is happening in heaven in Revelation 5:8?

  _____
  _____
  _____
  _____
  _____

> *"It is in the process of being worshipped that God communicates His presence to men."*
>
> — C.S. Lewis

Word Study - "Praise"

There are at least seven different Hebrew words that are translated "praise" in the Old Testament. In Psalm 22:3 King David says that God is enthroned in or inhabits the praises of God's people. The Hebrew word for praise in this verse is **tehillâ** (Strong's H8416). **Tehillâ** is connected in Scripture specifically to the idea of singing a new song to God (i.e. Psalm 40:3). Offering spontaneous worship, not just pre-written songs, is a powerful way to enter God's presence and move into presence-centered, joyful prayer.

ENJOYING PRAYER

Activation

Put on worship music for 10 minutes and sing to the Lord. Then, put on some instrumental music, open to Psalm 23, and sing the words to God.

Further Reading

Intercessory Worship by Dick Eastman

Scripture: The Language of Prayer

Big idea: *"The Bible is our source for understanding God's nature, His plan, and His heart." (pg. 70)*

1. The Bible Is A Doorway into Relationship with God

    - Read 2 Timothy 3:16. What is the source of the Bible? Who is the author? How does it claim to have originated? If the Bible is God's Word, how should you treat it?

    _____

    _____

    _____

    _____

    - Read John 5:39-40. Is it possible to study the Scriptures and not have a relationship with God? How do you think that happens, according to these verses? What do these verses teach you about how to approach the Bible?

    _____

    _____

    _____

    _____

2. Bible Meditation Leads to Supernatural Revelation

- Read Psalm 1:1-3. Does the idea of meditation seem weird to you? What specifically do these verses tell you to meditate upon? How often are you instructed to meditate on God's Word? What is promised to you if you meditate on God's Word?

- Read Matthew 6:7-8 in the New King James version. Does Jesus condemn all repetitive prayer? What specific kind of repetition does Jesus speak against? What makes repetition "vain"?

3. Biblical Intercession Ensures God Will Answer

- Read Isaiah 55:11 and Hebrews 4:12. What is God's promise regarding His Word? What kind of power is found in God's Word? Considering these verses, what do you think happens when we pray the promises found in God's Word?

SCRIPTURE: THE LANGUAGE OF PRAYER

> *"Pray the Bible, and you never again say the same old things about the same old things."*
>
> — C.S. Lewis

Word Study - "Law"

The Psalms open with an admonition to meditate on God's law day and night (Psalm 1:2). The Hebrew word for "law" in this verse is **tôrâ**. The **tôrâ**, or Torah, refers to the first five books of the Old Testament. This would have been the entirety of Scripture that the Hebrew people had when the Psalms were written. In other words, God's people are urged to meditate on the entirety of Scripture in order to be "like a tree planted by streams of water" (Psalm 1:3).

Activation

- Pray through John 3:16.
- Read it silently.
- Say it out loud.
- Write it down on a notepad or journal.
- Sing the verse to God (similar to last chapter's activation).
- Pray it. What does this verse say about God's nature? Praise Him for it. What does John 3:16 show us God has done? Thank Him for it. As you think about this verse, is there anything you need to confess or repent of? What can you ask God to help you with? Does this verse inspire you to pray for anyone else?

Further Reading

Praying the Bible by Wesley and Stacey Campbell

Listening: Hearing God's Voice in Prayer

Big idea: *"Prayer is always more fun when it is interactive and conversational."*
(pg. 91)

1. Praying is not talking *to* God but talking *with* God

   - Read Matthew 15:8. What are the people doing right? What are the people doing wrong? How did their hearts stay far from God while saying the right things?

   _____
   _____
   _____
   _____
   _____

   - Read John 10:27. What is Jesus doing in this verse? What two things are His people doing in this verse? If we are Jesus' sheep, what does this tell you about hearing God's voice?

   _____
   _____
   _____
   _____
   _____
   _____

ENJOYING PRAYER

- Read John 14:26. In this passage, what does Jesus promise the Holy Spirit will do? What will He bring to your remembrance? What does this verse say about how God may want to speak to you?

  _____

  _____

  _____

  _____

2. God speaks when we stop to listen

- Read I Kings 19:9-12. At what point did Elijah hear God's voice? How does verse 12 describe the voice of God? How does this story teach us to hear God's voice more clearly?

  _____

  _____

  _____

  _____

- Read Mark 1:35. In what kind of environment did Jesus pray? Why do you think Jesus prioritized solitude?

  _____

  _____

  _____

  _____

3. Hearing God's voice is subjective

- Read I Thessalonians 5:19-21. Does Paul believe that God can speak through the Holy Spirit? If God is speaking, why would you need to test what is being spoken? What are some ways to test what you think you hear from God?

  _____

LISTENING: HEARING GOD'S VOICE IN PRAYER

- Read Proverbs 12:15 and 19:20. What wisdom can you glean from these verses? How can wise counsel help you discern the voice of God?

> *"Recognize God's voice as spontaneous thoughts which light upon your mind."*
>
> — MARK VIRKLER

Word Study - "Word of God"

There are two Greek words in the New Testament that refer to God's "word" — **logos** and **rhema**. The **logos** of God refers both to the truth of Scripture (e.g. Hebrews 4:12) and to Jesus himself as the "Word made flesh" (John 1:14). The **rhema** of God refers to His spoken word or the voice of God (e.g. Acts 11:16). To truly know God requires that we both study the Scriptures, as well as hear God's voice by the Holy Spirit.

Activation

Set a timer for five minutes or sit near a clock. Turn off all phone notifications and sounds. Grab a notebook and a pen, but set it down beside you. Sit in silence and relax. Close your eyes and

ENJOYING PRAYER

remember that God is with you.. He may speak or He may not. But just be there with Him in stillness for five minutes. If you think He might be speaking to you, write it down. Share it with a mature believer in your life to help you discern if God was speaking. Consider making silence and stillness a regular part of your day.

Further Reading

4 Keys to Hearing God's Voice by Mark Virkler

Persistence: Staying Faithful in Prayer

Big idea: *"If we believe God is who He says He is and will do what He says He will do, then we will continue to come to Him faithfully in prayer." (pg. 98)*

1. God's word and prayer give us faith

   - Read Romans 10:17. Where does faith come from? Why does God's Word give you faith?

     _____
     _____
     _____
     _____

   - Read Mark 9:17-29. What did Jesus rebuke His disciples for in verse 19? What was Jesus' explanation for why He was able to cast out the demon in verse 29? What is the connection between the disciples' faithlessness and prayer?

     _____
     _____
     _____
     _____
     _____
     _____

ENJOYING PRAYER

2. Faith fuels our persistence in prayer

- Read Luke 18:1-8. What was Jesus' purpose in teaching this parable, according to verse 1? Why did Jesus bring up faith in verse 8? What does persistent prayer have to do with faith?

___

- Read Luke 2:36-38. Do you notice any similarities to this passage and the parable in Luke 18? What do you think Anna understood in her early years that allowed her to stay faithful in prayer for decades before Jesus was born?

___

- Read Matthew 21:22. What is the one condition that Jesus gives in this verse for having your prayers answered?

___

3. A delayed answer is not a reason to stop praying

- Read Daniel 10:2 and 10:10-14. How long had Daniel been praying? At what point was the angel dispatched? What caused the delay in the answer? What do you think kept Daniel steady for the 21 days?

___

PERSISTENCE: STAYING FAITHFUL IN PRAYER

- Read Psalm 56:8. What happens to the tears we cry before God? Read Acts 10:4. God said the prayers of Cornelius were like what to Him?

_____

_____

_____

- Read Revelation 5:8. Where are your prayers collected, according to this verse? Do you ever feel like your prayers are forgotten or lost? How does this verse encourage you to keep praying with persistence?

_____

_____

_____

_____

_____

"Our generation desperately needs to rediscover the difference between praying for and praying through. There are certainly circumstances where praying for something will get the job done... But there are also situations where you need to grab hold of the horns of the altar and refuse to let go until God answers."

MARK BATTERSON

Word Study - "Faith"

In Luke 18:8, Jesus asks if His people will be praying in faith when He returns. The Greek word translated "faith" in this verse is the word **pistis**. This word means what you would expect — a strong conviction or belief. However, Strong's concordance adds an insightful note to the end of their definition of **pistis**: "the character of one who can be relied on." This touches the heart of true biblical faith. It is not just believing the truth; it is trusting a Person. Our persistence in prayer is based on God's character more than the strength of our belief.

Activation

Take a promise that God has made to you, whether it is a biblical promise or a prophetic word, and find ways to remind yourself of it every day. Tape it to a mirror, or on your laptop, or on your dashboard. Every time you see it, pray for it. Be faithful.

Further Reading

God on Mute by Pete Greig

Part Three: Transformation through Enjoyable Prayer

Intercession: Partnership with God in Prayer

Big idea: *"Intercession is awakened through intimacy with God." (pg. 113)*

1. Jesus Is Our Intercessor

- Read Hebrews 7:25. How did Jesus already intercede for you? In what ways does He still make intercession for you? In what way does Jesus acting as an intercessor help you understand intercessory prayer?

  _____
  _____
  _____
  _____
  _____

- Read Psalm 2:8. Who is asking and who is being asked? Why would Jesus need to ask the Father for the nations? What does this say about God's nature and kingdom?

  _____
  _____
  _____
  _____
  _____

ENJOYING PRAYER

2. Every Christian Is an Intercessor

- Read Matthew 6:10. What is the ultimate goal of intercession? What does this verse teach you about how intercessory prayer works? Who should be praying for God's kingdom to come?

- Read I Timothy 2:1-2. What kinds of prayers should you pray? What is the ultimate goal of these prayers?

3. God Gives Intercessory Prayer Assignments

- Read John 16:24. According to this verse, why does Jesus want you to ask for things in prayer? If Jesus wants you to know when your prayers are answered, how specific should your prayers be?

- Read Romans 10:1. Who is Paul praying for in this verse? Despite that, who was Paul called to preach to (see Galatians 2:8)?

INTERCESSION: PARTNERSHIP WITH GOD IN PRAYER

- Read Romans 9:2-3. How does Paul feel about the Jewish people? How does this connect to his prayer in Romans 10:1? Does this give you an indication on how you can discern your own "intercessory prayer assignments"?

_____

_____

_____

_____

_____

_____

> *"...we have far too little conception of the place that intercession, as distinguished from prayer for ourselves, ought to have in the Church and the Christian life. In intercession our King upon the throne finds His highest glory; in it we shall find our highest glory too."*
>
> — ANDREW MURRAY

Word Study - "Intercession"

Isaiah 53:12 says Jesus "bore the sin of many, and makes intercession for the transgressors." The Hebrew word used in this verse is **paga**, which means to meet or encounter. In intercessory prayer, we cause two things to meet: the power of God and the person or thing for which we are praying. Just as Jesus the Intercessor reconciled us to God, in intercessory prayer we join with Christ in seeing God's love, power, presence, and kingdom encounter a broken world.

Activation

Take some time to discern if God has clearly given you any intercessory assignments. Reflect on your times of prayer, relationship with God, and personal history. Are there certain people groups or nations that stir your heart? Are there injustices that break your heart? Write these down. Ask

ENJOYING PRAYER

God to let you feel what He feels about these people and causes. Ask Him for grace to pray consistently for these assignments that He has given you.

Further Reading

Intercessory Prayer by Dutch Sheets

Tongues & Travail: Spirit-Filled Prayer

Big idea: *"To enter into the flow of intercessory partnership, we must embrace the gift of the Holy Spirit in our midst." (pg. 121)*

1. Joyful Prayer is Spirit-Filled Prayer

- Read Revelation 22:17. Who is the bride of Christ in sync with at the end of the age? What are they saying together?

  _____

  _____

- Read Galatians 5:22 and Acts 13:52. Who is the source of true joy?

  _____

- Read Romans 8:26. Who helps us pray when we feel weak? Have you invited the Holy Spirit to fill you and help you pray with more joy and effectiveness?

  _____

  _____

2. The Spirit Births God's Dreams Through Travailing Prayer

- Read Romans 8:20-26. What are the three things groaning in this passage? What is the cause of their groaning? These spiritual groanings are compared to what natural phenomenon? What is the role of the Holy Spirit in this birthing process?

  _____

  _____

ENJOYING PRAYER

_____

_____

_____

- Read Galatians 4:19. What is Paul groaning for in this verse?

_____

_____

- Read John 16:21. How does Jesus describe the process of childbirth? How does He describe the moments after childbirth? How does this relate to the idea of "birthing" God's purposes through prayer?

_____

_____

_____

_____

3. The Spirit Prays Through Us With The Gift of Tongues

- Read I Corinthians 13:1. What are the two categories of the gift of tongues mentioned in this verse? What are the tongues of men? What are the tongues of angels?

_____

_____

_____

_____

- Read I Corinthians 14:2-4 and Jude 20. When speaking in tongues, to whom are you speaking? What is the benefit of praying in tongues / praying in the spirit?

_____

_____

_____

TONGUES & TRAVAIL: SPIRIT-FILLED PRAYER

- Read I Corinthians 14:13-15. When praying in tongues, is it benefiting your mind or your spirit?

_____

_____

_____

> *"As you speak in tongues, you will find the Word of God opening to your mind, you will see an increase in divine appointments, and your thoughts and emotions will begin to carry the anointing of God."*
>
> — COREY RUSSELL

Word Study - "Spirit"

In I Corinthians 14, Paul connects the ideas of praying in tongues to praying "in the spirit." The Greek word used for spirit in this verse is **pneuma. Pneuma** is used in multiple ways to refer to the Holy Spirit, the spirits of people, and a movement of air (e.g. breath or the wind). When we pray "in the spirit," the Spirit (**pneuma**) of God fills our own spirits (**pneuma**) to cry out to God with the very breath (**pneuma**) that we first received from Him.

Activation

Ask the Holy Spirit to baptize you and fill you afresh. If you've never spoken in tongues, ask God for that spiritual gift. If you're struggling to speak in tongues, ask someone who already speaks in tongues to lay hands on you and pray. If you already speak in tongues, take 20 minutes (set a timer or watch the clock) and pray in tongues, even if you don't feel inspired. Take note of how you feel afterwards. Do you feel strengthened in your heart? Did God speak to you during that time?

Further Reading

The Glory Within and *The Gift of Tears* by Corey Russell

Fasting: Hunger for God Through Prayer

Big idea: *"In our Christian walk, sometimes the deepest joys come after doing the hardest things." (pg. 135)*

1. Fasting Regularly is Normal Christianity

- Read Matthew 6:16-18. Was Jesus trying to encourage His followers to fast? Did He expect them to be fasting regularly? Who should see you fasting, according to this passage? From where does one receive the rewards of fasting? How does Jesus' teaching impact your thoughts about fasting?

  _____
  _____
  _____
  _____
  _____

- Read Luke 18:12. How often did the Jewish religious leaders fast in Jesus' day? How often should Christians be fasting?

  _____
  _____
  _____
  _____

ENJOYING PRAYER

2. Fasting Expresses & Cultivates Hunger for God

- Read Matthew 9:14-15. What does Jesus call his disciples? What does he call Himself? When did he promise that his disciples would fast? Why would they fast at that time? How should this parable affect your approach to fasting?

- Read 2 Corinthians 12:10. When is God strongest in our life? Does fasting cause us to be strong or weak?

3. United Fasting and Prayer Releases God's Power and Blessing

- Read Joel 2:12-13. In this chapter, why is God calling His people to fast? What is the desired result from corporate fasting and prayer (see also Joel 2:28-29)? What gives God's people confidence that this might be effective?

- Read 2 Chronicles 7:14. What is the potential promise to God's people in this verse? What are the four conditions that must be met before that promise is fulfilled?

> *"To have found God and still to pursue Him is the soul's paradox of love."*
> A.W. TOZER

Word Study - "Mourning"

In Matthew 9, Jesus connects the idea of fasting and mourning. This seems to point back to the prophet Joel's call to return to God "with fasting, with weeping, and with mourning" (Joel 2:12). The Hebrew word used for mourning in that verse is **mispēd**, which literally means "wailing." This kind of prayerful mourning is not just an internal sadness but an overflowing yearning that leads to an outward cry of desperation. God is awakening that passion in His people who fast and pray — a "wailing" (**mispēd**) for revival and for the return of Christ.

Activation

Pick a day in the next week to skip lunch. During your normal lunchtime, read your Bible and pray. Soon after that, choose another day and wait until dinner before eating any solid food. Find a friend who will do this with you for accountability and encouragement. Consider making fasting a weekly discipline.

Further Reading

Shaping History through Prayer and Fasting by Derek Prince

Part Four:
The House of Enjoyable Prayer

Together: The Need for Corporate Prayer

Big idea: *"To step into our identity as Jesus' house of prayer, we have to stop viewing prayer as only individualistic." (pg. 149)*

1. The Place of Enjoyable Prayer Is In the House

- Read Matthew 21:13 where Jesus quotes Isaiah 56:7. When you think of a "house" of prayer, what comes to your mind? What is Jesus' house? Of all things, why do you think God says His house will be marked by prayer?

  _____
  _____
  _____
  _____
  _____

- Read the original quote again in Isaiah 56:7. Where exactly does God promise His people that they will experience joy?

  _____
  _____
  _____
  _____
  _____

ENJOYING PRAYER

2. Most Prayer in the Bible Is Corporate Prayer

- Read Acts 1:14. What were the followers of Jesus doing after He ascended to heaven? Were they doing it alone or together?

    _____

    _____

- Read Acts 2:42-47. After Pentecost, did the church continue to gather in corporate prayer and worship? As you read this passage, is the emphasis on the believers' personal relationship to God or their corporate relationship with God (see also Acts 4:32-35)?

    _____

    _____

    _____

3. We Pray Better when We Pray Together

- Read Hebrews 10:24-25. What should you be careful not to neglect? According to this passage, what is the impact of believers meeting together? As you near the return of Christ, should you gather with other Christians more often or less often?

    _____

    _____

    _____

    _____

- Read Matthew 18:19-20. What does Jesus' promise for those who gather in His name? How should these verses impact your approach to prayer?

    _____

    _____

    _____

    _____

> *"Sunday morning attendance shows how popular the church is. Sunday night shows how popular the preacher is. Wednesday prayer meeting shows how popular God is."*
>
> — LEONARD RAVENHILL

Word Study: "House"

The word used by Jesus in Matthew 21:13 for "house," when describing His house of prayer, is the Greek word **oikos**. This word not only means a physical dwelling but also a family. The **oikos** was both the place and the people. Therefore, the house of prayer described in Scripture does not simply refer to a physical location. It is the family of God joined in corporate prayer.

Activation

Attend a corporate prayer meeting. If your church has corporate prayer, get involved. If you don't know where to pray with others, visit houseofprayerhub.com to find a house of prayer near you. Schedule a time to visit the nearest prayer room.

Further Reading

Fresh Wind, Fresh Fire by Jim Cymbala

Unceasing: A Movement of Day & Night Prayer

Big idea: *"As you continue your personal journey into an enjoyable life of prayer, the revelation of a global prayer movement should inspire you with strength and courage." (pg. 162)*

1. Biblical Examples of 24/7 Prayer

- Read Revelation 4:8-11. How often are the four living creatures and 24 elders worshiping God? How do the angels worship "day and night" if there is no night in heaven (see Revelation 21:25)?

  _____

  _____

  _____

  _____

- Read I Chronicles 9:33. During what hours of the day did the musicians worship in David's tabernacle (see also Psalm 134)? Along with ministry to the Lord with praise, prayer, and prophecy, what additional responsibilities did the musicians have?

  _____

  _____

  _____

  _____

- Read Luke 2:37. How often was Anna worshiping and praying in the Temple?

  _____

ENJOYING PRAYER

- Read Luke 18:7. According to this verse, how often should God's people be praying? What does He promise to bring as a result of this kind of prayer?

  _____
  _____
  _____
  _____

2. God Has Promised to Fill the Earth with Day & Night Prayer

- Read Malachi 1:11. What are the incense and pure offerings in this prophecy? Where exactly does God promise that these offerings will be made on the earth?

  _____
  _____
  _____
  _____
  _____

- Isaiah 62:6-7. Who sets watchmen on the wall of prayer? How often are they crying out to God?

  _____
  _____
  _____

> *"Unceasing adoration and perpetual prayer have exploded all over the world. No longer is it only a few groups here and there with an outlandish vision."*
>
> — BILLY HUMPHREY

Word Study - "Continually"

When I Chronicles describes the Levites ministering at David's Tabernacle, it says that they ministered before the ark "continually." The Hebrew word for continually is **tāmîd** (Strong's H8548). It is not clear whether this indicates a continuous, 24/7 expression of worship, or simply a regular rhythm of daily worship. However, most uses of the word in the Scripture indicate something that is happening non-stop (Leviticus 6:13, Isaiah 60:11, etc.).

Prayer Prompts / Activations

Pray for prayer. Ask God to raise up 24/7 prayer and worship in your region. Make a commitment to give finances regularly to a ministry that prioritizes prayer. If you don't know where to give, go to houseofprayerhub.com for a map of prayer rooms.

Further Reading

Unceasing by Billy Humphrey

David's Tabernacle: How God's Presence Changes Everything by Matthew Lilley

CONCLUSION

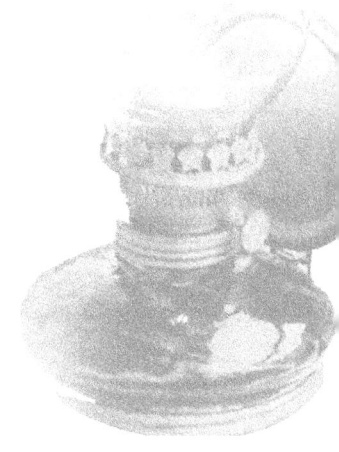

You're finished!

Congratulations on completing this study about joyful prayer. I hope during this time you have experienced deeper intimacy with God than ever before.

If you have rushed or skipped through any part of this guide, especially the activations, I encourage you to go through the study guide again more thoroughly. I am convinced that these biblical truths and simple steps of faiths will be transformative.

> *But be doers of the word, and not hearers only... James 1:22*

This study is complete, but your journey of enjoying prayer is only just beginning. It is your privilege as a child of God to walk in deep and enjoyable fellowship with the Father every day. Don't let this just be a season you look back on when you learned more about prayer. Set out to be a man or woman of prayer. To stay faithful in this new way of life, you will need to regularly refresh your mind with the biblical revelations found in these teachings. Take a few of the activations and turn them into habits. Keep learning. Keep growing. Keep going. Keep praying!

Finally, make sure you're not enjoying prayer alone. If you've gone through this study with a group, maintain relationships and keep encouraging one another in your walk with the Lord. Even if you studied *Enjoying Prayer* alone, share what you've learned with other brothers and sisters in Christ so that you can be encouraged and spread the truth that has impacted your life.

Before you conclude, take a moment right now to pray. Thank God for all He has done in your life. Thank Him for what He is teaching you. Thank Him for what He has shown you and how He's changing you. And ask Him for grace to enjoy prayer like never before.

QUOTE ATTRIBUTIONS

<u>Chapter One</u>
J. Daniel Hays and J. Scott Duvall, *God's Relational Presence* (Ada, MI: Baker Academic, 2019), 336.

<u>Chapter Two</u>
A. W. Tozer, *The Knowledge of the Holy* (New York: Harper Jubilee, 1961), 9.

<u>Chapter Three</u>
Jack Frost, *Experiencing Father's Embrace* (Shippensburg, PA: Destiny Image, 2006), 64.

<u>Chapter Five</u>
C. S. Lewis, "A Word About Praising," chapter 9 in *Reflections on the Psalms* (Edison, NJ: First Inspirational Press, 1994).

<u>Chapter Six</u>
C.S. Lewis, https://www.cslewisinstitute.org/resources/praying-the-bible/ (accessed 06-20-24).

<u>Chapter Seven</u>
Mark and Patti Virkler, *4 Keys to Hearing God's Voice* (Shippensburg, PA: Destiny Image, 2013).

<u>Chapter Eight</u>
Mark Batterson, https://www.markbatterson.com/praying-through/ (accessed 04-28-23).

<u>Chapter Nine</u>
Andrew Murray, https://www.gutenberg.org/files/29296/29296-h/29296-h.htm (accessed 03-28-24).

<u>Chapter Ten</u>
Corey Russell, *The Glory Within* (Shippensburg, PA: Destiny Image, 2013), 86.

<u>Chapter Eleven</u>
A. W. Tozer, *The Pursuit of God* (Harrisburg, PA: Christian Publications, Inc., 1976), 15.

<u>Chapter Twelve</u>
Leonard Ravenhill, https://www.gracegems.org/30/leonard_ravenhill_quotes.htm (accessed 03-28-24).

<u>Chapter Thirteen</u>
Billy Humphrey, *Unceasing* (Independently published, 2023), 1.

Check out these other titles from Presence Pioneers Media

10 DAYS
by Jonathan Friz

DAVID'S TABERNACLE
by Matthew Lilley

Available at
presencepioneers.org

To get updates and discounts on future book releases visit
media.presencepioneers.org or scan the QR code below

ABOUT THE AUTHOR

For over twenty years, Matthew Lilley has helped connect, equip and plant houses of prayer, praying churches and presence-centered communities. He is an author, worship leader, podcast host, and Bible teacher with a passion for God's presence, extravagant worship, and intercessory prayer. He founded Presence Pioneers in 2004 with a mission to build day and night worship and prayer for revival that touches the nations with the gospel of Jesus Christ. He is based in eastern North Carolina with his wife Shepard and their four children. Visit Matthew's blog and website at presencepioneer.com.

www.ingramcontent.com/pod-product-compliance
Lightning Source LLC
Chambersburg PA
CBHW040010080526
44586CB00028B/2946